Copyright © 2025 by Barbara Nelson Bennett

All rights reserved. No part of this publication may be reproduced, stored in a retrieval system, or transmitted in any form or by any means—electronic, mechanical, photocopying, recording, or otherwise—without the prior written permission of the publisher, except in the case of brief quotations used in reviews or scholarly works.

Published by New Being Books
Written by: Barbara Nelson Bennett
Cover Art by: Gabyriella Foster

Scripture quotations are taken from various versions of the Bible and are used with permission. All rights remain with the original publishers.

Unless otherwise noted, Scripture quotations are from the New International Version (NIV). ©1973, 1978, 1984, 2011 by Biblica, Inc.™ Used by permission. All rights reserved worldwide.

This is a work of nonfiction. Any similarities to real-life individuals, places, or events are purely coincidental unless explicitly stated.

ISBN: 979-8-99918479-4-0
Printed in The United States of America
First Edition, 2025

Author's note

It's hard out here.

Being a teen girl today isn't just challenging—it can feel like a battlefield. Between the pressure to look perfect, say the right things, keep up online, and figure out who you are, it's easy to feel like you're drowning in expectations, judgment, and confusion.

I've seen it. I've sat with girls who felt like they weren't enough. I've heard the stories of bullying, silent battles with shame, and moments of feeling completely misunderstood. As someone who works in education, I've watched girls walk into classrooms with their heads down, carrying the weight of words that never should've been spoken over them.

This book was born from those moments.

HEART FIRST was written for the girl who's trying her best to hold it all together. For the one who's questioning who she really is. For the girl who's smiling in the hallway but hurting inside. And for the girl who just needs someone to remind her of the truth:
You are more than what they say about you.

You are more than a bad day, a lost friendship, or a mistake.

You are seen. You are loved. And you belong.

This devotional is a safe space to get honest—with yourself and with God. Each day is a chance to breathe, reflect, and be reminded that your heart matters, your faith matters, and your future is filled with hope.

You don't have to be perfect to be loved by God. You just have to be real.

So here's your invitation: take it one day at a time. Let these pages walk with you through the hard, the healing, and the hope.

Start with your heart.

Barbara Nelson Bennett

To the girl who's been left out, laughed at, or labeled—

To the one who's ever felt too loud, too quiet, too much, or not enough—

To the girl who's sat alone in the cafeteria, walked the hall with her head down, or cried behind a closed door—

To the one who's been misunderstood, underestimated, overlooked, or bullied—
This devotional is for you.
You are not invisible.
You are not forgotten.

And you are not what they said about you.
You are seen, chosen, and deeply loved by the God who created you on purpose and for a purpose.
I pray these pages remind you that your heart matters, your voice matters, and your story is far from over.

HEART FIRST is for every girl who's been through the hard and is still standing.
This is your space to heal, grow, and remember who you truly are—one day at a time.

HEART FIRST
A DEVOTIONAL FOR TEEN GIRLS

Becoming the Girl God Designed You to Be

Barbara Nelson Bennett

DAY 1
Who God Says I Am - Understanding Identity in Christ

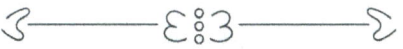

JOHN 15:16
You didn't choose me, I chose you. I appointed you to go and produce lasting fruit.

Let's be real—some days it feels like you're not enough. Not pretty enough, not funny enough, not smart enough. Maybe you've compared yourself to the girl with the perfect Instagram feed who posts the best pictures with the right lighting or filters. Maybe you even felt invisible in a room full of people. It can mess with your head.

But here's something that doesn't change no matter how you feel: God picked you. On purpose.

This isn't a participation trophy thing. God's not handing out compliments just to be nice. He made you on purpose for a purpose—and His voice matters way more than any like, comment, or rumor.

You're not an accident. You're not just "that quiet girl" or "the one who always messes up." You are chosen by the God who made the stars and still thinks the world needs one of you.

Believing that might take time, especially if people have told you otherwise. But the more you lean into His truth, the more the lies start to lose their grip.

REAL LIFE APPLICATION

Zara hated group projects—not because she couldn't do the work, but because no one ever picked her first. She felt like a backup. Then one night, while scrolling, she landed on a verse someone had posted: "You didn't choose me, I chose you." It felt personal. The idea that God saw her—really saw her—and picked her on purpose? It hit deep. She started writing truths on sticky notes and sticking them to her mirror: I'm chosen. I'm not forgotten. I matter. Slowly, the way she saw herself started to shift.

PRAYER

God, sometimes I feel like I'm not enough or like I don't really belong. Help me believe that You chose me for a reason. Let Your truth get louder than my insecurities, and remind me that who You say I am matters more than what anyone else thinks. **Amen.**

REFLECT

If you could read God's "profile" of you, what do you wish it said?

REFLECT

What lies do you catch yourself believing about your worth or identity?

REFLECT

What's one truth from today's devotional that you can write down and put where you'll see it often?

DAY 2
God Sees My Heart – Why Motives Matter

1 SAMUEL 16:7
People judge by outward appearance, but the Lord looks at the heart.

Let's talk about motives—what's going on inside when you do something. It's easy to say or do the right thing, especially when someone's watching. Smile at the teacher. Compliment a friend. Post a Bible verse. But if underneath it all, your heart is focused on being liked, getting praise, or secretly hoping someone else looks bad… God sees that too.

He's not impressed by fake kindness or surface-level "good girl" behavior. He's after something real: a heart that loves Him, not just a reputation that looks holy. The world teaches us to perfect our image. God calls us to check our hearts. That might mean being honest with yourself when you're helping just so you'll look helpful—or when you're saying sorry because you don't want to get in trouble, not because you're actually sorry.

God's not looking for perfect. He's looking for honest. And that's good news, because even when our hearts are messy, He can work with real.

REAL LIFE APPLICATION

Layla raised her hand in class to give an answer—after overhearing the girl next to her whisper it to someone else. She got credit for being "smart," and the teacher praised her. She acted cool, but the truth? She knew it wasn't hers. Later that day, the girl posted about "fake friends" and Layla's chest tightened. She didn't steal the answer to be mean—she just wanted to feel seen. Layla realized her insecurity pushed her to make a selfish choice, and that stung more than the guilt. That night, she didn't just pray for forgiveness—she asked God to show her why she craved attention so much in the first place.

PRAYER

God, I want my heart to match what I say and do on the outside. Show me when my motives are off—even when no one else sees it. Thank You for loving me even when I get it wrong. I want to be real with You. Change me from the inside out. **Amen.**

REFLECT

When was the last time you did something "right" for the wrong reason?

REFLECT

What's something you wouldn't want anyone to know was in your heart?

_____
_____
_____
_____
_____
_____
_____
_____
_____
_____
_____
_____
_____
_____
_____
_____
_____
_____
_____
_____
_____
_____
_____
_____
_____
_____
_____
_____

REFLECT

How can you start being more honest with God—even about the ugly stuff?

DAY 3
Choosing Kindness Even When It's Hard

LUKE 6:35

But love your enemies, do good to them, and lend to them without expecting to get anything back. Then your reward will be great.

Let's be honest: some people make it hard to be kind.

The girl who mocks your clothes. The friend who ghosted you. The guy who makes rude jokes at your expense. The teacher who calls you out every time you speak. It's easy to be kind when people are sweet, when your friends are loyal, when life feels safe. But kindness isn't a reaction—it's a choice. And sometimes, it's a battle.

Being kind doesn't mean being fake. It doesn't mean pretending things don't hurt. It means deciding not to let someone else's brokenness break you. It means keeping your peace instead of clapping back. It means choosing compassion when the world says "get even." Jesus showed kindness to people who betrayed, denied, and crucified Him. He didn't do it because they earned it—He did it because love isn't about who deserves it. It's about who needs it.

And sometimes, the person who needs it most… is the one acting the worst.

REAL LIFE APPLICATION

Janelle walked into lunch and saw the only open seat was next to the girl who'd spread rumors about her weeks ago. The same girl who called her "needy" in a group chat and blamed it on "just joking." Everything in Janelle wanted to grab her food and leave. Instead, she sat down, silent. After a minute, she said, "I know things have been weird, but I'm not trying to keep it that way." The girl looked surprised—then nodded. It didn't fix everything. They weren't besties by Friday. But it took *more* strength to be kind than it would've to stay cold. And that choice? It changed Janelle more than it changed the other girl.

PRAYER

God, help me be kind even when it's hard. Even when I'm hurt. Even when someone doesn't deserve it. Remind me that kindness is strength, not weakness. Teach me how to love the way You love—even when it costs me. **Amen.**

REFLECT

Who in your life is hard to be kind to right now—and why?

_____
_____
_____
_____
_____
_____
_____
_____
_____
_____
_____
_____
_____
_____
_____
_____
_____
_____
_____
_____
_____
_____
_____
_____
_____
_____
_____
_____

REFLECT

What do you usually do when you feel disrespected or hurt?

REFLECT

What might kindness look like in that situation—even if it's uncomfortable?

_____

DAY 4
Respecting Authority (Even When You Don't Feel Like It)

HEBREWS 13:17
Obey your leaders and submit to them, for they are keeping watch over your souls, as those who will have to give an account

Some adults don't listen. Some talk down to you like you're five. Some make rules that feel pointless. And let's be real—some just flat-out don't respect you. So why should you respect them?

Because God isn't asking you to respect authority because they always deserve it. He's asking you to respect authority because you belong to Him. It's not about agreeing with every rule or pretending every teacher, coach, or parent is right. It's about honoring the role—even when the person is difficult.

Respect doesn't mean staying silent if someone's being abusive or unsafe. That's not what God asks of you. But if you're just rolling your eyes at your mom because she said no to that party, or snapping at your teacher because you're in a bad mood—that's not about justice. That's about pride.

And pride is loud. Humility? That's what God listens to.

You might not always get it right. But every time you choose patience over attitude, every time you show grace instead of sarcasm—you're showing strength. Quiet, holy strength. And God sees it.

REAL LIFE APPLICATION

Amara's mom took her phone because she didn't do her chores—again. But it wasn't that simple. Amara had stayed up helping her younger siblings with homework the night before because her mom had to work late. She was exhausted, angry, and tired of always being "the responsible one." So when her mom grounded her, she snapped. "You don't even see what I do." Her mom paused, surprised. That night, Amara didn't apologize right away—but she prayed. And instead of yelling again the next morning, she calmly told her mom what she was feeling. It didn't erase the tension, but it opened a door. Sometimes, respecting authority means learning to speak truth with grace—even when your heart is tired.

PRAYER

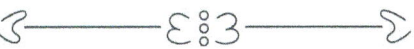

God, I don't always want to listen. Sometimes it feels unfair. But I want to live with a heart that honors You—even when it's hard. Teach me how to show respect without losing my voice. Help me trust You with my frustration. **Amen.**

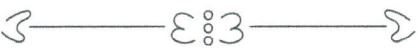

REFLECT

Who's the hardest authority figure for you to respect right now—and why?

REFLECT

How do you usually react when you feel misunderstood or overruled?

___

REFLECT

What's one small change you can make to respond with more maturity and grace?

_____
_____
_____
_____
_____
_____
_____
_____
_____
_____
_____
_____
_____
_____
_____
_____
_____
_____
_____
_____
_____
_____
_____
_____
_____
_____
_____

Words Have Power – Speaking Life, Not Gossip

PROVERBS 18:21
The tongue has the power of life and death, and those who love it will eat its fruit.

It starts small.
"She's so extra."
"He was totally checking her out."
"Don't tell anyone I said this, but…"

Gossip slips in like a whisper—but it hits like a wrecking ball.

You might not mean to tear someone down. Maybe it even feels justified. Maybe she really is toxic. Maybe he did do that thing. But here's the truth: when we talk about people behind their backs, we're not just passing time—we're passing judgment. And that judgment doesn't just stain them… it stains us. God gave your words the power to build or break. To heal or humiliate. Every time you speak, you're shaping someone's story—including your own.

So ask yourself:

Am I speaking life or just talking loud?

Because being "real" isn't about saying everything that comes to your mind. It's about choosing what doesn't need to be said. That's real strength. That's wisdom. That's love.

REAL LIFE APPLICATION

Tia was in a group chat with her three best friends when one of them sent a screenshot of a classmate's post and wrote, "Omg she's literally begging for attention." Everyone laughed and chimed in. Tia almost did too—but something stopped her. She remembered that same girl sitting alone in gym last week, hugging her knees. Tia deleted her message before sending it. Later, she DM'd the girl and just said, "Hey, you good?" That tiny decision? It haunted her—in a good way. Because for the first time, she realized kindness wasn't silence. It was speaking life when it would've been easier to stay popular.

PRAYER

God, help me guard my words. Teach me to speak with purpose and kindness. When I want to gossip, remind me of the power I hold. Help me use my voice to lift people up—not tear them down. **Amen.**

REFLECT

When have you said something you wish you could take back? What happened?

REFLECT

What does "speaking life" mean to you in your own friend group?

_____
_____
_____
_____
_____
_____
_____
_____
_____
_____
_____
_____
_____
_____
_____
_____
_____
_____
_____
_____
_____
_____
_____
_____
_____
_____

REFLECT

Who's someone you can speak life over today—in person or online?

_____
_____
_____
_____
_____
_____
_____
_____
_____
_____
_____
_____
_____
_____
_____
_____
_____
_____
_____
_____
_____
_____
_____
_____
_____
_____
_____
_____

DAY 6
Dealing with Anger God's Way?

EPHESIANS 4:26
In your anger do not sin: Do not let the sun go down while you are still angry.

Let's be real—anger isn't always loud.
Sometimes it's slamming a door.
Sometimes it's going silent.
Sometimes it's smiling in someone's face while thinking, I'm done with you.

Anger is real. Jesus felt it. God isn't asking you to never be angry. He's asking you not to let it own you. Because when anger takes the driver's seat, it'll wreck everything—your peace, your friendships, even your view of yourself.

God's way isn't to bury your feelings or fake forgiveness. He wants your anger brought to Him, not buried inside you or exploded on others. When you bring Him your real feelings—rage, bitterness, confusion—He won't shame you. He'll steady you. He'll shape that fire into strength instead of destruction.

God isn't scared of your anger. But He doesn't want it turning you into someone you're not.

REAL LIFE APPLICATION

Rae's dad promised he'd come to her championship game. She kept scanning the stands, hoping. He didn't show. Again. That night, when he tried to call, she declined. The next morning, she snapped at her mom for no reason. She didn't even cry—just felt numb. But at youth group, her small group leader asked one question: "Have you told God the truth about how mad you are?" Rae didn't know what to say. That night, she broke down and told God everything. The words came out ugly and raw—and freeing. That prayer didn't fix her dad. But it started healing her.

PRAYER

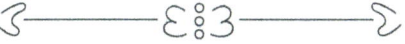

God, I'm angry—and sometimes I don't know what to do with it. Help me bring my anger to You instead of lashing out or shutting down. Teach me how to feel without sinning. Heal the places in me that still hurt. **Amen.**

REFLECT

What are you angry about right now—even if it feels small or "unimportant"?

___
___
___
___
___
___
___
___
___
___
___
___
___
___
___
___
___
___
___
___
___
___
___
___
___
___
___
___
___
___

REFLECT

What would it look like to invite God into your anger instead of pushing Him away?

_____
_____
_____
_____
_____
_____
_____
_____
_____
_____
_____
_____
_____
_____
_____
_____
_____
_____
_____
_____
_____
_____
_____
_____
_____
_____
_____
_____

DAY 7
God Is Always With Me (Even at School)

JOSHUA 1:9
Have I not commanded you? Be strong and courageous. Do not be afraid; do not be discouraged, for the Lord your God will be with you wherever you go.

You walk into school, and it's like stepping onto a stage where everyone's watching—judging what you wear, how you talk, who you sit with. You're expected to be chill, confident, smart, funny… but not too much of anything. It's exhausting.

And it can feel like God is… distant. Like He belongs in your quiet time or church, not your 3rd period math class or lunch table drama.

But He is there.

When you're sitting alone and wondering why your friends are suddenly cold—He's there.

When you fail the test you studied all night for—He's there.

When a teacher embarrasses you in front of the whole class—He's there.

When you pray quietly at your locker and wonder if anyone notices—He's definitely there.

You don't need perfect prayers or spiritual music playing to experience God's presence. Just your real, raw self. Wherever you go—yes, even there—He's walking in with you.

REAL LIFE APPLICATION

Mikayla had a panic attack in the middle of biology class. Not dramatic—just her heart racing, hands shaking, vision tunneling. She didn't tell anyone. Just asked to go to the bathroom, locked the stall door, and cried. In that moment, she didn't quote Scripture. She didn't even pray words. She just whispered, "God, please." That was it. But somehow, she felt like she wasn't alone. It wasn't magic—it was presence. She stood up, wiped her face, and made it through the rest of the day. God didn't "fix" everything, but He showed up. Right in the middle of the mess.

PRAYER

God, help me remember You're with me—not just at church or home, but at school, when things feel awkward or overwhelming. Walk beside me in every hallway and sit with me in every class. I need You everywhere. **Amen**.

REFLECT

When do you feel closest to God—and when do you feel farthest from Him?

REFLECT

What's one school moment that made you feel alone or unseen?

_____
_____
_____
_____
_____
_____
_____
_____
_____
_____
_____
_____
_____
_____
_____
_____
_____
_____
_____
_____
_____
_____
_____
_____
_____
_____
_____
_____

REFLECT

What would it change if you actually believed God was with you all day, even at school?

_____
_____
_____
_____
_____
_____
_____
_____
_____
_____
_____
_____
_____
_____
_____
_____
_____
_____
_____
_____
_____
_____
_____
_____

DAY 8
Friendship That Honors God

1 CORINTHIANS 15:33
Do not be misled: 'Bad company corrupts good character.

Friendship is powerful. It can make you feel like you belong—or like you're not enough.

The people closest to you help shape your voice, your choices, and even how you see yourself.

So the question isn't just "Do I have friends?"—it's "Are these friendships building me up or breaking me down?"

God doesn't call you to be friends with everyone. But He does call you to love people well. A friendship that honors God doesn't mean being perfect, fake, or spiritual 24/7. It means honesty, loyalty, encouragement, accountability—and calling each other out when you're slipping, not hyping up bad behavior just because you don't want to lose your spot in the group chat.

You don't need a crowd. You need people who speak life, not shade. Who celebrate you, not secretly compete with you. Who love Jesus and are growing—even if they're not there yet.

And most importantly: Are YOU that kind of friend?

REAL LIFE APPLICATION

Alyssa loved hanging with her squad—they were funny, fearless, and made her feel seen. But when one of the girls got dumped, the group went full savage. They stalked his socials, made TikToks throwing shade at his new girl, and even dared Alyssa to leave hate comments. She laughed along at first… but it started feeling gross. One night she couldn't sleep, so she prayed and felt God nudge her: "This isn't who you are." The next day, she quietly left the group chat. It hurt. But it also healed. She didn't lose friends. She lost noise—and made space for real ones.

PRAYER

God, help me find and be the kind of friend who honors You. Show me when to step closer and when to let go. I want friendships that help me grow, not ones that pull me away from who I'm becoming. **Amen.**

REFLECT

What kind of friend are you most of the time—encouraging, critical, loyal, flaky? Be real.

___

REFLECT

Is there someone in your life who pulls you closer to God just by how they live?

_____
_____
_____
_____
_____
_____
_____
_____
_____
_____
_____
_____
_____
_____
_____
_____
_____
_____
_____
_____
_____
_____
_____
_____
_____
_____

REFLECT

What's one small step you can take to be a better friend today?

_____
_____
_____
_____
_____
_____
_____
_____
_____
_____
_____
_____
_____
_____
_____
_____
_____
_____
_____
_____
_____
_____
_____
_____
_____

DAY 9
What Does It Mean to Obey?

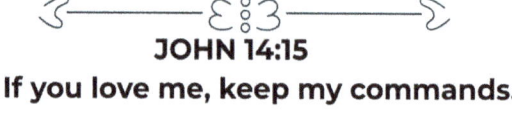

JOHN 14:15
If you love me, keep my commands.

Let's be honest: the word obey isn't cute. It sounds like rules, restrictions, and being told "no" when you just want freedom.
But here's the thing—God's not after robotic obedience. He's after your heart.

When Jesus says, "If you love me, obey me," He's not demanding fake perfection. He's inviting real trust.

Obedience isn't about following rules so God won't be mad. It's about following Jesus because you believe He knows more than you do. Even when it's hard. Even when it costs you. Even when you don't get applause for it.

It might mean walking away from something that feels good but isn't good for you.

It might mean owning your mistake instead of lying.

It might mean forgiving someone who doesn't deserve it.

Obedience isn't always loud. Sometimes it's quiet, behind the scenes, nobody clapping for you—but Heaven noticing.

REAL LIFE APPLICATION

Jordan was in love. Or so she thought. Her boyfriend was older, charming, and knew exactly what to say. But when he started pressuring her to send pics she wasn't comfortable with, everything in her heart said, "This isn't right." She didn't want to be that girl—judged, called dramatic, or left. But one night, she said no. He ghosted her. She cried for days. But in the silence, she also felt peace. Real peace. God whispered, "That was obedience. I saw that." And that meant more than any text from him ever could.

PRAYER

God, help me obey You even when it's not easy or popular. Help me trust that Your way leads to life—even when I don't understand. Give me strength to walk away from anything that pulls me from You. **Amen.**

REFLECT

What's one area of your life where obedience to God feels hard right now?

REFLECT

Do you believe God's commands are for your good—or do they feel like control?

_____
_____
_____
_____
_____
_____
_____
_____
_____
_____
_____
_____
_____
_____
_____
_____
_____
_____
_____
_____
_____
_____
_____
_____
_____
_____
_____
_____

REFLECT

What would obedience look like in your actual choices this week?

DAY 10
The Beauty of Forgiveness (Giving & Receiving)

EPHESIANS 14:15

Be kind and compassionate to one another, forgiving each other, just as in Christ God forgave you.

Forgiveness is beautiful—but let's not pretend it's easy.

It's hard to forgive someone who doesn't say sorry.

It's hard to admit you were the one who messed up.

It's hard to move on when the pain still sits in your chest like a knot.

But here's the truth: forgiveness isn't saying what they did was okay. It's saying, "I'm choosing not to let this own me anymore."

And on the flip side—when you need forgiveness, you don't earn it by doing the most. You receive it by being honest, humble, and real. God's already made the first move. His forgiveness isn't temporary or conditional. It's complete. He forgives with grace—and calls us to do the same.

It doesn't mean forgetting. It means releasing.

It doesn't mean pretending. It means healing.

And that's where the beauty is.

REAL LIFE APPLICATION

Tay got humiliated in front of everyone when her best friend exposed a secret she swore she'd keep. Tay was done. Cold. Blocked. Weeks later, the girl sent a long, real apology—but Tay wasn't ready. She kept replaying what happened. But then her youth leader asked, "Do you want peace or payback?" That hit. Tay didn't feel like forgiving, but she didn't want to stay bitter either. So she prayed. She journaled. She gave space. And eventually—she forgave. Not because it didn't hurt, but because she didn't want to carry the weight anymore.

PRAYER

Jesus, thank You for forgiving me—over and over. Help me forgive like You do, even when it's hard. Heal the places in me that still feel raw. Teach me how to let go without losing myself. Jesus, thank You for forgiving me—over and over. Help me forgive like You do, even when it's hard. Heal the places in me that still feel raw. Teach me how to let go without losing myself. **Amen.**

REFLECT

Who's someone you're struggling to forgive? Why is it hard?

REFLECT

Have you been avoiding owning a mistake that hurt someone else?

REFLECT

What would it look like to forgive yourself the way God forgives you?

_____
_____
_____
_____
_____
_____
_____
_____
_____
_____
_____
_____
_____
_____
_____
_____
_____
_____
_____
_____
_____
_____
_____
_____
_____
_____
_____

DAY 11
Being Different is a Blessing (Standing Out for the Right Reasons)

ROMANS 12:2

Don't copy the behavior and customs of this world, but let God transform you into a new person by changing the way you think

It can feel safer to blend in than to stand out.

To laugh at the joke you didn't find funny.

To post what gets likes, not what's real.

To go along with the group—even when your gut says, "This isn't me."

But being different isn't a flaw. It's a calling. If you follow Jesus, you're not supposed to look like everyone else. You were made to stand out—not for attention, but for intention. To bring light where there's darkness. To walk in truth even when it's awkward. To be kind when everyone else is savage.

You might not get invited. You might be misunderstood. But you'll also discover something the crowd never will—freedom. Purpose. Peace. That quiet confidence that says, "I'm not who the world wants—I'm who God called."

REAL LIFE APPLICATION

Ari always felt "too much" for some people. Too Jesus-y. Too deep. Too different. At school, her faith made her a target—some girls mocked her for not cursing or partying. She hated it. She cried more nights than she admitted. But then a younger student DM'd her: "Thank you for being real. I've been scared to live my faith, but watching you gave me courage." Ari realized she wasn't just being different—she was making a difference. And it was worth it.

PRAYER

God, when I feel left out or weird for doing things Your way, remind me that being different is part of my purpose. Help me be bold, not bitter. Strong, not stubborn. Let my life reflect You—even when it's hard. **Amen**.

REFLECT

What makes you feel different from people around you? Do you see it as a burden or a blessing?

REFLECT

Have you ever hidden your faith or your values to fit in? Why?

REFLECT

What's one way you can stand out for the right reasons this week?

_____
_____
_____
_____
_____
_____
_____
_____
_____
_____
_____
_____
_____
_____
_____
_____
_____
_____
_____
_____
_____
_____
_____
_____

Why Lying Hurts More Than It Helps

PROVERBS 12:22
The Lord detests lying lips, but he delights in those who tell the truth.

Let's keep it real: lying is easy.

It can get you out of trouble, make you look better, or avoid awkward drama.

But here's what no one tells you—lying always costs more than it gives.

Every lie puts a crack in your peace.

You start worrying about getting caught. You forget what version of the story you told.

You wonder if people like you or just the version of you they think they know.

Even "small" lies shape you. And they slowly build a wall between you and God—because God is truth.

When you lie, you're saying, "I don't trust God enough to handle the truth."

But when you're honest—even when it's ugly—you invite freedom in.

God doesn't need your perfect image. He wants your honest heart.

REAL LIFE APPLICATION

Maya lied about where she was going. Said she was at a sleepover when she was really at a party. She didn't plan on drinking, but it happened. And when her mom found out, it blew up. Trust shattered. Maya felt stupid, ashamed, and alone. She thought the lie would protect her—but it actually broke more than it saved. Months later, after a brutal conversation, her mom said, "I'm not mad you made a mistake. I'm hurt you didn't trust me with the truth." That stuck with her. She realized honesty invites help—lies isolate. She started rebuilding from there.

PRAYER

God, help me be brave enough to be honest—even when it's hard. Heal the parts of me that feel like I need to hide. Teach me to love truth like You do. **Amen.**

REFLECT

Why do you think lying feels easier than telling the truth sometimes?

_____
_____
_____
_____
_____
_____
_____
_____
_____
_____
_____
_____
_____
_____
_____
_____
_____
_____
_____
_____
_____
_____
_____
_____
_____
_____

REFLECT

What lie have you told recently that you need to confess—to God or someone else?

REFLECT

What would change in your relationships if you chose truth over pretending?

_____
_____
_____
_____
_____
_____
_____
_____
_____
_____
_____
_____
_____
_____
_____
_____
_____
_____
_____
_____
_____
_____
_____
_____
_____
_____

DAY 13
Jesus Listens When I Pray

PSALM 145:18
The Lord is close to all who call on him, yes, to all who call on him in truth.

Have you ever prayed and felt... nothing?
No lightning. No voice from heaven. Just silence.
Maybe you've thought, "Does God even hear me?"

You're not alone. But the truth is—Jesus always listens. He doesn't need fancy words. He doesn't need you to have it all together. He just wants your honest voice.

God isn't like people who only listen halfway or scroll while you talk. He leans in.

He's not bored. He's not annoyed. He's with you.

Even when your prayers feel small. Even when you pray through tears, or don't have the words at all. Prayer isn't just about getting what you ask for—it's about who you're talking to.

The One who knows your heart better than you do. The One who's never too busy.

REAL LIFE APPLICATION

Lena used to pray just to check a box. Before meals. At bedtime. Quick and quiet. But when her dad got sick, she didn't know what to say anymore. She stopped praying altogether for a while—until one night she just broke down and cried, "God, I don't know how to do this." No Bible words. No filter. Just raw pain. And that was the night she felt something shift. Not in her situation—but in her heart. Peace. Unexplainable, but real. She realized prayer wasn't about performance—it was about presence.

PRAYER

Jesus, thank You for always listening. Even when I feel lost, silent, or unsure, You don't turn away. Help me talk to You like I would a friend—honest and real. Teach me to trust that You're near. **Amen.**

REFLECT

Have you ever felt like God wasn't listening to your prayers? What was that like?

REFLECT

What kind of prayers feel "safe" to pray—and which ones feel scary or too honest?

_____
_____
_____
_____
_____
_____
_____
_____
_____
_____
_____
_____
_____
_____
_____
_____
_____
_____
_____
_____
_____
_____
_____
_____
_____

REFLECT

Try writing a prayer that's completely unfiltered. What would you say to Jesus?

_____
_____
_____
_____
_____
_____
_____
_____
_____
_____
_____
_____
_____
_____
_____
_____
_____
_____
_____
_____
_____
_____
_____
_____
_____
_____

DAY 14
When You Feel Left Out

PSALM 27:10
Even if my father and mother abandon me, the Lord will hold me close.

Being left out hurts in a way that's hard to explain.

It's the ache of not being picked. Not being invited. Not being seen.

You replay it—"Did I do something wrong?"

You scroll past the party pics. Laugh at their inside jokes even though they sting.

You pretend you're fine—but it eats at you.

Here's what's real: even when people forget you, God doesn't.

Even when friends leave you out, God holds you close.

Jesus gets it. He was betrayed by His closest friends, misunderstood, even abandoned on the worst day of His life.

So when you whisper, "This hurts," He doesn't just hear you—He understands.

Being left out doesn't mean you're less.

It might just mean you're being protected, set apart, or redirected.

And while that doesn't erase the sting, it does remind you: you're not invisible to the One who matters most.

REAL LIFE APPLICATION

Jasmin's whole friend group started hanging out without her after she said no to something she wasn't comfortable with. She watched her group chat go silent, while the girls posted TikToks together. She felt replaced. Unwanted. She cried alone in the school bathroom more than once. One day in church, a guest speaker said, "God doesn't just give friends—He gives the right ones." That stuck. Slowly, God brought new people into her life who valued her boundaries and didn't make her feel like a backup option. It took time, but now she sees it: being left out opened space for something better.

PRAYER

God, when I feel invisible or unwanted, remind me that I'm deeply known by You. Fill the lonely places with Your love. Help me wait for the friendships that reflect Your heart. Amen.

REFLECT

When was the last time you felt left out? How did you handle it?

REFLECT

Do you believe God sees you even when others don't? Why or why not?

_____
_____
_____
_____
_____
_____
_____
_____
_____
_____
_____
_____
_____
_____
_____
_____
_____
_____
_____
_____
_____
_____
_____
_____

REFLECT

How can you show someone else today that they belong?

DAY 15

What to Do When You're Tempted to Be Mean

ROMANS 12:21

Don't let evil conquer you, but conquer evil by doing good

Let's be honest—sometimes being mean feels justified.

She embarrassed you. He spread lies. They left you out. And now? You've got the perfect comeback ready. You can ghost them, clap back, or make them feel the sting you felt.

But here's the catch: reacting in anger might feel good for a minute—but it doesn't heal anything.

Meanness might win the moment, but it loses in the long run.

You were made for more than just "getting even." You were made to reflect Jesus—even when it's hard. Being kind when it hurts isn't weak. It's powerful.

It says, "I don't have to become what hurt me." It keeps your heart soft when the world tries to harden it.

And it turns the spotlight off revenge and onto God—who sees everything.

REAL LIFE APPLICATION

Tori found out someone she trusted shared private stuff behind her back. She was done. She had receipts and could've destroyed the girl's reputation in one post. But something tugged at her. She waited. Prayed. Sat with her feelings instead of blasting them. A week later, the girl apologized. Turns out she was dealing with a lot of shame and insecurity. Tori still set boundaries, but didn't ruin her. She said, "If I had gone off, I would've lost who I am trying to become." Choosing kindness didn't erase the pain—but it protected her peace.

PRAYER

Jesus, You showed kindness even when people were cruel. Help me do the same. When I want to lash out, slow me down. Make me strong enough to be kind—even when I don't feel like it. **Amen.**

REFLECT

What situation is making you feel tempted to be mean right now?

_____
_____
_____
_____
_____
_____
_____
_____
_____
_____
_____
_____
_____
_____
_____
_____
_____
_____
_____
_____
_____
_____
_____
_____

REFLECT

What's one small way you can choose kindness instead of revenge?

REFLECT

How does showing kindness actually protect you, not just others?

_____
_____
_____
_____
_____
_____
_____
_____
_____
_____
_____
_____
_____
_____
_____
_____
_____
_____
_____
_____
_____
_____
_____

Day 16

God's Love Never Changes

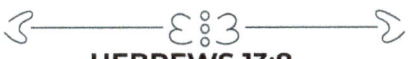

HEBREWS 13:8
Jesus Christ is the same yesterday, today, and forever.

Some days you feel like God must really love you. You're kind, you read your Bible, you help a friend.

Other days? Not so much. You mess up, lash out, skip prayer, or scroll through stuff you know you shouldn't.

You start thinking: "Maybe God's love for me goes up and down, too."

But here's the truth: God doesn't love like people do.

He doesn't ghost you when you fail.

He doesn't love you more when you "get it right."

He doesn't get tired of you—even when you get tired of yourself.

God's love isn't a mood. It's a promise.

It held you yesterday. It holds you today. It will still be holding you tomorrow.

When you feel worthy. When you feel like a mess. When you're confused, numb, angry, or on fire for Him.

His love doesn't flinch.

REFLECT

Do you ever feel like God's love for you depends on your behavior? Why?

_____
_____
_____
_____
_____
_____
_____
_____
_____
_____
_____
_____
_____
_____
_____
_____
_____
_____
_____
_____
_____
_____
_____
_____
_____
_____
_____
_____

REFLECT

What's one truth about God's love that you want to hold onto today?

_____
_____
_____
_____
_____
_____
_____
_____
_____
_____
_____
_____
_____
_____
_____
_____
_____
_____
_____
_____
_____
_____
_____
_____
_____

REFLECT

How would your life change if you really believed God's love never changes?

_____
_____
_____
_____
_____
_____
_____
_____
_____
_____
_____
_____
_____
_____
_____
_____
_____
_____
_____
_____
_____
_____
_____
_____
_____

DAY 17

You Are Not Too Young to Be Used by God

1 TIMOTHY 4:12

Don't let anyone think less of you because you are young. Be an example to all believers in what you say, in the way you live, in your love, your faith, and your purity.

Maybe you've thought, "When I'm older… then God can use me."

Once I have more confidence.

Once I stop messing up.

Once I'm taken seriously.

But God doesn't look at your age—He looks at your heart.

Throughout the Bible, God used young people to shake the world:

- David was a teen when he faced Goliath.
- Mary was likely your age when God chose her to carry Jesus.
- Josiah became king at 8 and led a whole nation back to God.

Being young isn't a barrier—it's a superpower. You've got energy, boldness, passion, and a fresh voice this world needs to hear.

God's not waiting until you've got it all together. He's ready now.

So don't shrink. Don't wait.

Live boldly. Love big. And lead like someone who knows who she belongs to.

REAL LIFE APPLICATION

At 13, Leila started a TikTok account just to share random encouragement and Bible verses. She figured maybe a few girls from school would see it. Within a year, her videos about battling anxiety, choosing joy, and trusting God hit over 100,000 likes. Girls started DM'ing her asking for prayer and advice. She didn't feel qualified, but she stayed honest and real—and pointed them back to Jesus. "I'm not perfect," she said, "but if God can use this awkward 8th grader with a cracked iPhone screen, He can use anybody."

PRAYER

God, thank You for seeing value in me, even when I feel too young or not enough. Use my words, actions, and heart to make a difference—right here, right now. **Amen**.

REFLECT

Have you ever felt "too young" to do something meaningful for God?

REFLECT

What is one small way you can lead or serve someone this week?

REFLECT

What gift or passion has God given you that you could use now, not later?

How to Build a Soft Heart, Not a Hard One

EZEKIEL 36:26

And I will give you a new heart, and I will put a new spirit in you. I will take out your stony, stubborn heart and give you a tender, responsive heart.

When life hurts, your heart starts building walls.
You stop trusting.
You stop caring.
You tell yourself: "If I don't feel, I won't get hurt."
And at first, it works. You feel numb instead of broken.

But over time, that numbness spreads—and it starts to choke out the good stuff too. Joy. Empathy. Love.

You weren't created to live with a hard heart. God made you with a soft heart—a heart that loves deeply, feels fully, and heals even after being cracked.
It's not weak to stay tender.
It's bold.
Because it means choosing to stay open even when people let you down.
It means letting God in—not just to fix you, but to feel with you.
God never asks you to fake it. He just asks you to hand Him the pieces so He can shape your heart back into something soft, strong, and whole.

REAL LIFE APPLICATION

Dana's dad walked out when she was ten, and she promised herself she'd never let anyone close enough to hurt her again. By 14, she was known for being "cold." No one could touch her, emotionally. But one day at youth group, a leader shared how hard hearts can protect, but they can't connect. That line broke something in her. She sat in her room that night and cried for the first time in years. "I didn't even know I still had feelings," she said. That was the start of letting God soften what life had hardened.

PRAYER

God, I don't want to live with a hard heart. Help me feel again, love again, trust again. Make my heart tender—strong enough to care and soft enough to let You in. **Amen.**

REFLECT

Have you ever felt yourself shutting down emotionally to avoid being hurt?

___

REFLECT

What would it look like to let God begin softening your heart again?

_____
_____
_____
_____
_____
_____
_____
_____
_____
_____
_____
_____
_____
_____
_____
_____
_____
_____
_____
_____
_____
_____
_____
_____
_____
_____
_____
_____

REFLECT

Is there someone you need to forgive—not for them, but for your own healing?

_____
_____
_____
_____
_____
_____
_____
_____
_____
_____
_____
_____
_____
_____
_____
_____
_____
_____
_____
_____
_____
_____
_____
_____
_____
_____

DAY 19

What Real Strength Looks Like (Hint: It's Not Attitude)

2 CORINTHIANS 12:9

My grace is all you need. My power works best in weakness

Our world confuses attitude with strength. It tells you:
- Be savage, not soft.
- Be loud so they don't ignore you.
- Don't cry. Don't feel. Don't need anyone.
- But God flips the script. Real strength? It doesn't yell the loudest. It doesn't come from pretending nothing touches you.

Real strength is choosing gentleness when you want to snap.

Real strength is showing up when your anxiety says stay in bed.

Real strength is saying "I need help" instead of acting like you've got it all together.

Jesus was the strongest person to ever walk the planet. But He wasn't arrogant. He wasn't cold. He wept, served, forgave, and stood up for others—all while being rooted in who He was.

So next time someone says, "You're so strong," ask yourself—is it because of my pride or my courage to be real?

REAL LIFE APPLICATION

Ava always had the reputation of being "the tough one." She'd clap back, roll her eyes, and shut people down with sarcasm before they got too close. But the truth? She was just scared of being seen as weak. One day during worship at a retreat, she felt God whisper, "You don't have to carry all of this by yourself." For the first time, she cried—in public—and didn't feel ashamed. After that, she started asking for prayer, letting her guard down, and encouraging other girls to be real too. "Turns out, vulnerability takes more guts than pretending," she said.

PRAYER

God, help me let go of the fake strength I've used to protect myself. Make me strong like You—full of love, grace, and truth. I want to be bold and soft. **Amen**.

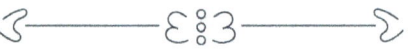

REFLECT

In what ways have you pretended to be "strong" to hide what you're really feeling?

_____
_____
_____
_____
_____
_____
_____
_____
_____
_____
_____
_____
_____
_____
_____
_____
_____
_____
_____
_____
_____
_____
_____
_____
_____
_____
_____
_____
_____

REFLECT

What do you think God says real strength looks like?

REFLECT

How can you show strength this week by choosing honesty, kindness, or courage?

_____
_____
_____
_____
_____
_____
_____
_____
_____
_____
_____
_____
_____
_____
_____
_____
_____
_____
_____
_____
_____
_____
_____
_____

Making Wise Choices

JAMES 1:5

If any of you lacks wisdom, you should ask God, who gives generously to all without finding fault, and it will be given to you.

Some choices are obvious:
Should I cheat? No.
Should I be kind? Yes.
But other choices are messy:
- Should I keep this friendship or walk away?
- Do I speak up or stay silent?
- Should I post this, or is it doing too much?

Wisdom isn't just about knowing right from wrong—it's knowing what honors God when the answer isn't clear.

The good news? You don't have to figure it out alone.

God isn't hiding wisdom. He's offering it.

He speaks through His Word, through the Holy Spirit, and sometimes even through people who love Him and love you.

But you have to be willing to pause long enough to ask Him. And humble enough to actually listen.

REAL LIFE APPLICATION

Maya was asked to be part of a group chat that mostly roasted people at school. It wasn't full-on bullying, but it definitely wasn't kind. She didn't want to seem boring or "too Christian," but she also knew it felt wrong. She asked her older cousin what she'd do, then sat on her bed and literally prayed, "God, I don't wanna be lame, but I don't wanna be fake either. What should I do?" She left the chat. It cost her some clout—but it earned her peace. "I still get invited to stuff," she said. "But now it's on my terms, not theirs."

PRAYER

God, help me slow down when I'm making choices. Teach me to ask for wisdom and actually listen for Your answer. I want to make decisions that reflect You—not just what feels good in the moment. **Amen.**

REFLECT

What's one decision you're facing that you need God's wisdom for?

REFLECT

Who are people in your life that give godly advice?

___

REFLECT

What's one way you can pause and pray before deciding something this week?

_____
_____
_____
_____
_____
_____
_____
_____
_____
_____
_____
_____
_____
_____
_____
_____
_____
_____
_____
_____
_____
_____
_____
_____
_____

DAY 21

The Holy Spirit Helps Me Every Day

JOHN 14:26

But the Helper, the Holy Spirit, whom the Father will send in My name, He will teach you all things and bring to your remembrance all that I said to you

You weren't meant to do life with God without God.

Yet so many girls try to follow Jesus on their own strength—trying to be "good enough," to say the right things, to not mess up. Exhausting, right? But Jesus didn't just leave us with a rulebook. He gave us the Holy Spirit—God living in us.

The Holy Spirit isn't a ghost or a churchy word we only talk about at camp. He's real.

And He helps you:
- Remember truth when lies scream loud.
- Find peace when your anxiety is high.
- Hold your tongue when you're about to snap.
- Speak up when someone needs encouragement.
- Make decisions that bring life, not regret.

The more you get to know the Holy Spirit, the more you realize you're not alone in trying to live this life. You've got help. Every day.

REAL LIFE APPLICATION

Jasmine was always scared of praying out loud, even in small groups. Her heart would race, and she'd feel like everyone else sounded way more "spiritual." But at a youth retreat, she felt like God nudged her to say a short prayer for a girl who was crying. Her hands shook, but she did it. "I don't even remember what I said," she admitted later. "But she hugged me after and said it was exactly what she needed." Jasmine realized that wasn't her strength—it was the Holy Spirit helping her in real time.

PRAYER

Holy Spirit, thank You for being with me. Help me hear You, trust You, and lean on You every single day. I don't want to do life without You. I need Your help. **Amen.**

REFLECT

Have you ever felt the Holy Spirit prompting you to do or say something?

_____
_____
_____
_____
_____
_____
_____
_____
_____
_____
_____
_____
_____
_____
_____
_____
_____
_____
_____
_____
_____
_____
_____
_____
_____
_____
_____

REFLECT

In what areas of your life do you need His help right now?

_____
_____
_____
_____
_____
_____
_____
_____
_____
_____
_____
_____
_____
_____
_____
_____
_____
_____
_____
_____
_____
_____
_____
_____

REFLECT

What would it look like to start your day inviting Him in?

_____
_____
_____
_____
_____
_____
_____
_____
_____
_____
_____
_____
_____
_____
_____
_____
_____
_____
_____
_____
_____
_____
_____
_____
_____
_____
_____

DAY 22

Jealousy Steals Joy

PROVERBS 14:30
A peaceful heart leads to a healthy body; jealousy is like cancer in the bones

Let's be real: jealousy sneaks in fast.
You were feeling fine... until she got the part.
Until their post blew up.
Until he texted her back and not you.
 It's not just about wishing you had what someone else has—it's about believing you don't measure up unless you do. And that lie will drain you.
Jealousy makes you see people as threats instead of friends.
 It makes you scroll in silence, clapping for no one, and secretly hoping someone else fails—just so you don't feel behind.
 But here's the truth: someone else's win doesn't mean your loss.
 God's goodness isn't limited. He's big enough to write your story and theirs without canceling either. When you feel jealousy rising, don't just shove it down. Take it to Jesus. Ask Him to remind you of what's already yours—and help you cheer for others like you mean it.

REAL LIFE APPLICATION

Leah was genuinely happy when her friend got the lead in the school play—at least that's what she told everyone. But later that night, she spiraled: "Why not me? I worked just as hard." She didn't sleep. She almost quit drama club altogether. But instead, she texted her friend, "Proud of you. I'm sad for me, but proud of you." Her friend responded with so much kindness, it caught her off guard. "I felt peace right away," Leah said. "It wasn't about the part—it was about not feeling left behind."

PRAYER

God, You know when jealousy creeps into my heart. Help me catch it early and come to You instead of stewing in comparison. Remind me of who I am in You—and teach me to celebrate others with a full heart. **Amen.**

REFLECT

When do you feel most tempted to compare yourself to others?

REFLECT

What's something about your life right now that you can thank God for?

REFLECT

Who can you genuinely celebrate today, even if it's hard?

_____
_____
_____
_____
_____
_____
_____
_____
_____
_____
_____
_____
_____
_____
_____
_____
_____
_____
_____
_____
_____
_____
_____
_____
_____
_____
_____
_____

DAY 23

What to Do When You Mess Up

1 JOHN 1:9

If we confess our sins, He is faithful and just and will forgive us our sins and purify us from all unrighteousness

Messing up can make you want to run.
Run from people.
Run from God.
Run from the truth.
But here's what shame doesn't want you to know: God's love doesn't disappear when you do.
God doesn't roll His eyes when you confess. He leans in closer. He's not surprised, not disappointed beyond repair, and definitely not done with you.

You don't need to pretend you're fine or overcompensate by doing "extra" good things. You just need to be honest.

Confess it. Own it. Bring it to Him.

God is faithful. And He's not just in the business of forgiving—He's in the business of restoring.

REAL LIFE APPLICATION

Nina started secretly vaping because her older cousin did. She told herself it was "no big deal" until she got caught—and disappointed her mom badly. The worst part? She felt like she couldn't even pray anymore. "I felt fake, like God didn't want to hear from me." But one night she broke down crying and told God everything. She didn't sugarcoat it. Didn't make promises she couldn't keep. Just admitted it. "I felt this weird peace after, like He already knew, and just wanted me back." That's grace.

PRAYER

Jesus, I've messed up. I don't want to hide anymore. I need Your forgiveness and Your help. Thank You that You never give up on me. Teach me how to grow from this, not stay stuck in it. **Amen**.

REFLECT

Is there something you've been keeping from God out of shame or fear?

REFLECT

How does it feel to know God isn't shocked or done with you?

_____
_____
_____
_____
_____
_____
_____
_____
_____
_____
_____
_____
_____
_____
_____
_____
_____
_____
_____
_____
_____
_____
_____
_____

REFLECT

What would "coming clean" look like for you today?

God's Plan for My Body and Mind

1 JOHN 1:9

Do you not know that your bodies are temples of the Holy Spirit, who is in you, whom you have received from God? You are not your own; you were bought at a price. Therefore honor God with your bodies.

Your body and your mind are not mistakes.
They're not ugly. Not weak. Not "too much" or "not enough."
They're gifts—sacred space where God dwells. That means your body deserves care—not because of how it looks in pictures, but because of who made it.
And your mind? It deserves protection—because what you think about becomes how you live.
The world tells you to "do whatever feels good," but God's plan is way better. He wants you to flourish—physically, mentally, emotionally. That means setting boundaries, resting, eating well, thinking true things, and treating yourself with the same compassion you give others.
You don't have to be perfect. But you do have to start seeing yourself as someone worth caring for.

REAL LIFE APPLICATION

Kayla used to skip lunch a lot—telling people she "wasn't hungry." Truth? She hated how her stomach looked in gym class. She felt like smaller girls had it easier. But one night, she read this verse and something clicked. "If I'm a temple, why am I starving it?" It didn't magically fix her body image, but it made her pause. She started being honest—with herself and with God. And slowly, she began feeding her body like someone worth loving.

PRAYER

God, thank You for my body and mind—even when I struggle to see them as good. Teach me how to care for what You've given me. Help me think true thoughts, rest when I need to, and live like I'm someone You love—because I am. **Amen.**

REFLECT

What lies have you believed about your body or mind?

REFLECT

What's one way you can honor God with your body this week?

REFLECT

What's one negative thought you need to replace with truth?

_____
_____
_____
_____
_____
_____
_____
_____
_____
_____
_____
_____
_____
_____
_____
_____
_____
_____
_____
_____
_____
_____
_____
_____
_____
_____

DAY 25

How to Be a Leader, Not a Follower

1 TIMOTHY 4:12

Don't let anyone look down on you because you are young, but set an example for the believers in speech, in conduct, in love, in faith and in purity

Being a leader isn't about having the loudest voice or the most followers.

It's about influence—and you already have some. People are watching how you treat others. What you post. What you laugh at. What you ignore. And every time, you're teaching them what matters to you. It's easier to go with the crowd. To laugh at the joke that crosses the line. To let the group make the choice so you don't have to.

But God didn't call you to blend in—He called you to stand out with love and integrity.

Being a leader means walking away when things get toxic, even if everyone stays. It means sticking up for someone who's not popular. It means being confident in who you are, even if that makes you different. Leadership isn't about being perfect—it's about choosing courage, especially when it's inconvenient.

REAL LIFE APPLICATION

Jade was the only one who didn't go along with the "prank" in her group chat. They were planning to post an embarrassing photo of a girl they didn't like, just to mess with her. Everyone else laughed, even the ones who usually didn't. Jade said, "This isn't funny," and left the chat. The next day, two other girls told her they were glad she spoke up—they didn't feel right either but were afraid to say something. Jade didn't just stand alone—she showed others how to do it too.

PRAYER

God, help me be bold when it's easier to blend in. Make me a leader who walks in truth, kindness, and strength. Show me what it looks like to lead with love—not pride. And give me courage to do what's right, even when it's not popular. **Amen.**

REFLECT

When have you felt pressured to follow the crowd?

REFLECT

What does godly leadership look like in your world (school, friend group, online)?

_____
_____
_____
_____
_____
_____
_____
_____
_____
_____
_____
_____
_____
_____
_____
_____
_____
_____
_____
_____
_____
_____
_____
_____
_____
_____
_____
_____

REFLECT

Who is someone you admire for standing out—and what can you learn from them?

DAY 26

What Is Real Beauty

1 PETER 3:3–4

Your beauty should not come from outward adornment... Rather, it should be that of your inner self, the unfading beauty of a gentle and quiet spirit, which is of great worth in God's sight.

There's a version of beauty that the world pushes hard.

Clear skin. Perfect body. Curated outfits. Effortless hair. A certain way to laugh, pose, filter.
But there's another kind of beauty—the kind that doesn't fade, doesn't depend on lighting, and doesn't require constant validation. It's the kind that radiates from someone who knows who she is, and more importantly, Whose she is.

Real beauty looks like confidence that isn't loud.

Kindness that doesn't need applause.

Strength that doesn't belittle others.

Peace in your skin—even when it's imperfect.

God doesn't say beauty is bad—He just wants you to see it the way He does: from the inside out.

REAL LIFE APPLICATION

Tasha got addicted to Facetune. Every picture she posted had tweaks—nose a little smaller, waist a little thinner, skin totally smooth. She told herself, "It's just editing, everyone does it." But the more she filtered her pics, the worse she felt without them. One day she heard a speaker say, "If you have to shrink yourself to feel worthy, something's broken—and it's not your face." That hit her. She started posting unedited selfies—not for clout, but for freedom. It was scary, but freeing. And for the first time, she felt real.

PRAYER

God, I confess I've believed lies about beauty. Help me see myself the way You do—fearfully and wonderfully made. Grow in me the kind of beauty that reflects You—gentle, strong, real. **Amen.**

REFLECT

What standards of beauty have you tried to live up to—and how has that made you feel?

_____
_____
_____
_____
_____
_____
_____
_____
_____
_____
_____
_____
_____
_____
_____
_____
_____
_____
_____
_____
_____
_____
_____
_____
_____
_____
_____
_____

REFLECT

How does God's definition of beauty challenge or encourage you?

_____
_____
_____
_____
_____
_____
_____
_____
_____
_____
_____
_____
_____
_____
_____
_____
_____
_____
_____
_____
_____
_____
_____
_____
_____
_____
_____

REFLECT

What's one thing you can do to start embracing your real, God-given beauty?

_____
_____
_____
_____
_____
_____
_____
_____
_____
_____
_____
_____
_____
_____
_____
_____
_____
_____
_____
_____
_____
_____
_____
_____
_____

DAY 27

Letting Go of Shame

PSALM 34:5
Those who look to him are radiant; their faces are never covered with shame.

There's a difference between guilt and shame.
Guilt says, "I made a mistake."
Shame whispers, "I am a mistake."
Shame sticks to you like a shadow, dragging your past into your present. It'll tell you you're too messed up, too far gone, too dirty for grace.

But Jesus doesn't speak with shame.

He convicts—but He also forgives. He corrects—but then He restores.

He doesn't rub your face in the dirt—He lifts it.

The enemy wants you to keep hiding, but God is calling you to step into the light where healing begins.

You don't have to carry what Jesus already paid for.

REAL LIFE APPLICATION

Sam slept with her boyfriend and broke up with him two weeks later. She felt gross and angry—mostly at herself. At youth group, when the leader talked about grace, Sam wanted to disappear. "That's for good girls," she thought. Later, she opened up to a trusted mentor. Instead of judging, the woman shared her own story of past regret—and how Jesus met her in the middle of it. Sam realized that God wasn't trying to shame her but rescue her. That conversation was the start of her healing.

PRAYER

God, I've been carrying shame like a backpack of bricks. I want to be free. Help me believe that Your grace really covers everything. Heal the parts of me that still feel broken. Replace shame with peace. **Amen**.

REFLECT

Is there something you've been ashamed of that you haven't talked to God about yet?

_____
_____
_____
_____
_____
_____
_____
_____
_____
_____
_____
_____
_____
_____
_____
_____
_____
_____
_____
_____
_____
_____
_____
_____
_____
_____

REFLECT

What would change if you really believed you were forgiven?

REFLECT

Who is a safe, trusted person you can talk to for support?

_____
_____
_____
_____
_____
_____
_____
_____
_____
_____
_____
_____
_____
_____
_____
_____
_____
_____
_____
_____
_____
_____
_____
_____

DAY 28

Helping Others Even When No One Sees

MATTHEW 6:4
And your Father who sees in secret will reward you.

In a world where everything's posted, shared, and liked—doing something good without getting noticed feels… pointless.

But here's the truth: God sees what others miss. When you pick up someone's books after they drop, and no one claps.

When you check on the quiet girl in class.

When you pray for a friend who doesn't even know it.

When you serve without the spotlight—that's kingdom work.

God cares less about how loud your kindness is and more about how real it is.

He sees the hidden. He honors the humble.

You don't need a stage to live a life that matters.

REAL LIFE APPLICATION

Lena brought extra snacks to school—not for herself, but because she noticed one kid never brought lunch. She didn't announce it, didn't post about it, didn't even tell her friends. When someone asked, she just said, "I had extra." That kid never said much, but after a few weeks, he started smiling more. A year later, he wrote her a note saying, "You were the first person who made me feel seen." Lena didn't even know her quiet act had that much weight. But God did.

PRAYER

Lord, help me love and serve others even when it's quiet. Remind me that You see everything—and that nothing done in love is ever wasted. Make my heart more like Yours. **Amen**.

REFLECT

Do you feel like your small acts of kindness matter? Why or why not?

_____
_____
_____
_____
_____
_____
_____
_____
_____
_____
_____
_____
_____
_____
_____
_____
_____
_____
_____
_____
_____
_____
_____

REFLECT

Who in your life could use help or encouragement right now?

REFLECT

What's one thing you can do this week that no one else needs to know about—but God will see?

_____
_____
_____
_____
_____
_____
_____
_____
_____
_____
_____
_____
_____
_____
_____
_____
_____
_____
_____
_____
_____
_____
_____
_____
_____

DAY 29

Peace Over Drama

ROMANS 12:18
If it is possible, as far as it depends on you, live at peace with everyone.

Drama loves to invite you in.

She starts small: a side comment, a screenshot, a "did you hear about…"

Before you know it, there's group chats blowing up, friendships cracking, and stress you didn't ask for. But you don't have to RSVP to the drama party.

God calls us to something better—peace. Peace doesn't mean being a doormat.

It means choosing maturity over mess.

Walking away instead of snapping back.

Clarifying, not assuming.

Blessing people, even when they're being petty.

When you carry peace, you protect your energy, your joy, and your witness. Let the world chase chaos —you don't have to.

REAL LIFE APPLICATION

Elise was in a friend group that thrived on drama. Every week, someone was "out," someone was "fake," and there was always a fight brewing. She realized she went to school tired—not from homework, but from keeping up. One night, after another round of tears and texts, she muted the chat and spent the evening journaling and praying. The next day, she started hanging with people who didn't live off gossip. It felt weird at first, but peaceful. For the first time in months, she didn't feel anxious just walking into school.

PRAYER

God, give me the courage to walk away from drama. Help me be a peacemaker, not a pot-stirrer. Fill me with Your calm when everything around me feels loud. Let me be known for peace, not pettiness. **Amen**.

REFLECT

Are you more drawn to peace or drama lately? What do your habits show?

REFLECT

What boundaries might you need to set to protect your peace?

_____
_____
_____
_____
_____
_____
_____
_____
_____
_____
_____
_____
_____
_____
_____
_____
_____
_____
_____
_____
_____
_____
_____
_____

REFLECT

Who in your life models peaceful strength—and what can you learn from them?

_____
_____
_____
_____
_____
_____
_____
_____
_____
_____
_____
_____
_____
_____
_____
_____
_____
_____
_____
_____
_____
_____
_____
_____
_____
_____
_____
_____

DAY 30

Trusting God with My Future

JEREMIAH 29:11
For I know the plans I have for you,' declares the Lord, 'plans to prosper you and not to harm you, plans to give you a hope and a future

When people ask, "What do you want to be when you grow up?" do you panic inside?

Maybe you've got big dreams—but they scare you.

Maybe you have no clue—and that scares you more.

The pressure to figure everything out can feel crushing. But here's what God wants you to know: you don't have to have all the answers to be in His plan.

God isn't waiting for you to draw a perfect blueprint.

He's asking you to take the next right step—and trust Him with the rest.

He sees what you can't. He's not overwhelmed by your questions, your detours, or your fears.

When you give Him your future, you'll find peace—even in the unknown.

REAL LIFE APPLICATION

Kyla had her whole future mapped out—she was going to be a vet, move out by 18, and start her dream life. Then her grades slipped, her family went through a financial crisis, and suddenly, her timeline unraveled. She cried one night praying, "What do You want from me, God?" It wasn't instant, but over time, she started noticing how much she loved working with younger kids at church. Now, she's studying to be a child therapist—something she never saw coming. "God redirected me," she says. "And I'm so glad He did."

PRAYER

Lord, my future feels big and unknown. Help me stop trying to control every part of it. Remind me that Your plan is better than mine. Lead me one step at a time. I want to walk in peace, not panic. **Amen**.

REFLECT

What fears or pressures do you feel when you think about your future?

REFLECT

Do you believe God is capable of guiding you—even if you feel lost?

_____
_____
_____
_____
_____
_____
_____
_____
_____
_____
_____
_____
_____
_____
_____
_____
_____
_____
_____
_____
_____
_____
_____
_____
_____
_____

REFLECT

What's one small step of trust you can take today?

_____
_____
_____
_____
_____
_____
_____
_____
_____
_____
_____
_____
_____
_____
_____
_____
_____
_____
_____
_____
_____

DAY 31

Starting Over with God's Grace

LAMENTATIONS 3:22–23

The steadfast love of the Lord never ceases; his mercies never come to an end; they are new every morning

Sometimes you just want to hit reset.

You said the wrong thing. You snapped at someone. You slipped back into something you promised God you were done with.

And the guilt? It hits hard.

But grace isn't a one-time offer. God's grace meets you right where you are—again and again.

You don't have to earn a second chance.

You don't have to "clean yourself up" before coming back.

Jesus already paid for your mess-ups. And His love doesn't change just because you stumbled.

Every morning is a fresh page.

You are never too far gone to begin again—with God.

REAL LIFE APPLICATION

Malia was doing great—reading her Bible, going to youth group, praying. Then she started sneaking around with a guy who didn't treat her right. Her friends tried to warn her, but she pulled away. After it all fell apart, she felt ashamed and too "dirty" for God. She stopped praying. One night at youth camp, she broke down in tears during worship and whispered, "God, I'm sorry." That night, she felt something she hadn't in months—peace. She realized God wasn't done with her. He never was.

PRAYER

God, thank You for never giving up on me. Even when I mess up, You still love me. Help me let go of shame and start fresh with You. I'm so grateful for grace that never runs out. **Amen**.

REFLECT

Have you been holding on to guilt that God already forgave?

_____
_____
_____
_____
_____
_____
_____
_____
_____
_____
_____
_____
_____
_____
_____
_____
_____
_____
_____
_____
_____
_____
_____
_____
_____
_____

REFLECT

What keeps you from believing you can start over with Him?

REFLECT

What's one step you can take today to walk in His grace instead of your shame?

_____
_____
_____
_____
_____
_____
_____
_____
_____
_____
_____
_____
_____
_____
_____
_____
_____
_____
_____
_____
_____
_____
_____
_____
_____
_____
_____
_____

www.ingramcontent.com/pod-product-compliance
Lightning Source LLC
Chambersburg PA
CBHW071434160426
43195CB00013B/1901